point

M.C. HAMMER & VANILLA ICE

THE HIP-HOP NEVER STOPS!

By Nancy E. Krulik

SCHOLASTIC INC.
New York Toronto London Auckland Sydney

Acknowledgments

The author would like to thank the following people
for their help and encouragement with this book:
M.C. Hammer, Vanilla Ice, Lauren Margulies, Violet Brown, Leslie Gould at Shock Ink, Linda Lou
McCall at Bust It Management/Production, Shalon
Cunningham, Daniel Burwasser, Deborah Thomp-
son, and especially Jean Feiwel, who really knows
how to catch a rising rap star on the way up!

Photo Credits
Cover Photos: M.C. Hammer © Vinnie Zuffante/Star File Vanilla Ice ©
Michael Lavine. **Inside Photo Spread:** *Page 1:* M.C. Hammer © Vinnie
Zuffante/Star File. *Page 2:* Vanilla Ice © Michael Lavine. *Page 3:* M.C.
Hammer (both) © Ralph Dominguez/Globe. *Page 4:* Vanilla Ice © Michael
Lavine. *Page 5:* M.C. Hammer (top) © Mike Guastella/Star File (bottom)
© Chuck Polin/Star File. *Page 6:* Vanilla Ice (both) © Michael Lavine. *Page
7:* M.C. Hammer (top left) © Todd Kaplan/Star File (top right) © Jeff Mayer/
Star File (bottom) © Jeff Mayer/Star File. *Page 8:* Vanilla Ice ©
T. Kaplan/Star File.

ISBN 0-590-44980-X

12 11 10 9 8 7 6 5 4 3 2 1   1 2 3 4 5 6/9

Printed in the U.S.A.   01

First Scholastic printing, February 1991

Contents

Contents

M.C. HAMMER

JAMMIN' HIS WAY TO THE TOP!

1.
It's Hammer Time!

"Timing had a lot to do with [my success]. I feel the time was right for a different style of music that was more danceable and that appealed to both young and old."

If M.C.Hammer is right, and success is mostly in the timing, then the 1990s are definitely HAMMER TIME! With two hit albums, two MTV video awards, two American Music awards, a best-selling home video, and a sold-out nationwide tour behind him, Hammer's hot on a rap roll.

When Capitol Records released Hammer's debut album, *Let's Get It Started*, in 1988, the recording company expected the album to have limited success. Back then, Capitol was trying to break into the rap world, and Hammer's combination of hip-hop and pop was right up the record label's alley. Capitol hoped the record would sell well enough to find a spot on Billboard's rhythm-and-blues or top 100 charts. No one (except Hammer, of course) *ever* expected *Let's Get It Started* to spawn three top 10 singles *and* sell the million and a half records, tapes, and CD's it did! In fact, the album was such a success that *Billboard* magazine named Hammer the number one rap artist of 1989 and named him the number two new black artist of 1989.

But that wasn't enough for M.C. Hammer. He was determined to take over all the charts in 1990. And he did! His second album, *Please Hammer Don't Hurt 'Em*, was released in early 1990. It slammed right past albums by mega-stars Madonna and New Kids on the Block to hit number one on the *Billboard* pop, and rhythm-and-blues charts. *Please Hammer Don't Hurt 'Em* held tight to the number one pop spot for 21 weeks. No album had done that since Michael Jackson's *Thriller*!

People in the music business are stunned by M.C. Hammer's success. Certainly none of the industry's hotshots ever would have predicted him to be the biggest selling recording artist of 1990. After all, rappers aren't supposed to have that big an audience. But Hammer did become the biggest selling artist of the year — in fact, thanks to the incredible sales of *Please Hammer Don't Hurt 'Em*, M.C. Hammer was the only musical artist of 1990 to pass the triple platinum mark!

Maybe that's because Hammer is more than just another rapper. He's a full-blown entertainer known not just for the raps he busts but for his slammin' fancy footwork and amazing stage shows. And little by little, Hammer is changing the shape of the rap world. More and more, rappers are adding a little dancing to their shows.

"Rap, the way I'm presenting it, has no limitations," Hammer declares proudly. "My music has as much singing and dancing as any pop record."

And what a dancer Hammer is! The man can move! In rap circles he's known as "the Paula Abdul of rap." And considering all of the awards Paula's won for her choreography, that's quite a compliment. Hammer's smooth style of dancing has become his trademark — so much so that the rapper has taken out insurance, just in case he can't dance anymore!

It's not hard to get Hammer to talk about

his career. The Oakland homeboy is proud of the successes he's had. But Hammer is more than just talk. His passion for charity work is well known. Hammer has never forgotten the poor California neighborhood he came from. And to prove it, Hammer has hired lots of his old homies to work at Bust It Management/Production, the music company he created. That took a lot of guts, especially since some of those homeboys have spent some time in jail.

But the one thing Hammer absolutely will not talk about is his personal life.

"As far as my personal life goes, I don't make that public," he explains. "It's very hard for me to have a private life. Once you lose your privacy, you know what it is to have it. So I let my family maintain their privacy."

But even without talking about his family, Hammer's never hard up for words. All he has to do is get talking about his newly found mega-stardom.

"I'm able to conquer all avenues with this particular style of rap — pop-oriented, full of melodies and harmonies," he says. "I want to be able to achieve the success of a major artist, I don't want anything to get in my way!"

2.
The Oaktown Homie
at Home

East Oakland, California, is one tough
neighborhood. Drugs, gangs, and violence
are everywhere. It was into that part of
Oaktown that Stanley Kirk Burrell was
born in 1963. Someday little Stan would
grow up to be M.C. Hammer, the most
famous rapper of all time, but back in the
early 1960s he was just the youngest boy
in the Burrell family. Stan had eight brothers and sisters, and the whole family was
crammed into a three-bedroom apartment
in the projects.

For the first few years of his life, young
Stan's father, Louis, managed a poker club
in the neighborhood. But the Burrells di-
vorced when Stan was just five years old,
and his mother, Betty, was forced to take
a lot of low-paying jobs, just to keep the

cash flowing in. Still, all that hard work wasn't enough to always properly feed and clothe the Burrell kids.

"We were definitely poor," Hammer says now. "Welfare, government-aided apartment building, the whole thing."

Living in poverty can have two effects on people. Some people give up on ever making anything of themselves. They turn to drugs and crime. They usually wind up in prison.

"Of the fifteen guys I hung with on my block, ten wound up in San Quentin [a California prison]," Hammer says sadly.

But the projects can also make people work hard to move up in the world. And that's the route Hammer took.

"Growing up in poverty gave me added incentive to strive for a better life," Hammer explains.

Deep down, Hammer always knew that music would help him get that better life. So, it was on the streets of East Oakland that Hammer gave his very first public performance — when he was only three years old!

"I saw James Brown at the Apollo on TV when I was three or four years old," Hammer says. "I did a whole routine of

'Please, Please, Please,' falling to the ground and crawling!"

Hammer learned many of his slammin' dance moves on TV while he was growing up. His idols were the dancers the Nicholas Brothers; James Brown, Marvin Gaye, and other soul singers. Hammer spent a lot of time watching those soul singers on TV and copping their smooth moves. Then he would go out to elementary school talent shows and try out the moves on the people.

As a kid, dancing and singing weren't Hammer's only obsessions. What Hammer loved more than anything was baseball — especially his home team, the Oakland A's. Hammer would do almost anything to get tickets to see his team play. Mostly he would hang out in the parking lot, doing his James Brown riff, hoping one of the A's would slip him a ticket to the game.

One summer afternoon, when Hammer was eleven, the kid was definitely in the right place at the right time. Hammer was doing some smooth dance moves in the A's parking lot when he was spotted by Charlie O. Finley, the owner of the Oakland A's. Charlie Finley was known for being a real grump — he didn't like anyone! But for some reason, Charlie Finley was knocked out by Hammer's funky footwork. The young kid with the fast-moving feet actually made Charlie smile! And to Hammer's surprise, Charlie O. Finley himself invited Hammer to come watch the game.

"He said, 'Why don't you come to the game as my guest, and bring your friends, too?'" Hammer recalls. After a while, Hammer became a regular guest at the A's home games. And then he became part of the team! Charlie Finley hired him as a batboy. When he got to be about 16 years old, Hammer became an office assistant. Sometimes, when there was no school in session, Hammer was allowed to travel with the team, taking Charlie Finley's personal phone calls.

Hammer says going around the country on those road trips helped him learn a lot about people. "I learned to adapt and get along. I saw how other people live and feel. Maybe that's what separates me from most other rappers who only understand one way of life."

The players on the team were really nice to the young kid from the streets of Oakland. In fact, it was a baseball player named Pedro Garcia who gave young Stan Burrell an early nickname, "Little Hammer."

"Garcia was the first guy to say, 'You look like the Hammer,'" M.C. Hammer says. "He meant I reminded him of Hank Aaron."

Home-run king Hank Aaron had the nickname "Hammer" long before M.C. Hammer did. After Garcia gave him the nickname, everyone on the team called Stan Burrell "Little Hammer." Later on, when he needed a stage handle because he was rapping full time, Hammer dropped the "little" and added the M.C. M.C. means "master of ceremonies" or "leader of the band" in rap slang.

After he graduated from high school, Hammer figured he'd take a shot at becoming a pro baseball player. He took a tryout with the San Francisco Giants. But Hammer just couldn't make the grade. So, he decided to try his luck in college. He headed off to East Los Angeles College to get a degree in communications.

Hammer stayed in college for a year. But then he ran out of money. He was forced to head back to Oakland. He had no job and no money coming in. Hammer knew that couldn't last forever. It was time for him to decide what to do with his life.

Back home, Hammer found that in East Oakland the only guys on the streets with any money were the guys who were dealing drugs. And although Hammer never got involved with the drug scene, he has admitted that the idea did cross his mind.

"I never touched the stuff," Hammer vows. "But one morning I sat up in bed and thought about how I had lived a clean, positive life, and suddenly there I was, actually considering being reduced to no more than an average drug dealer."

That very morning, Hammer hopped out of bed, ran to the nearest Navy recruiting office, and took a test to enlist in the Navy. Hammer got all 50 questions on the test right. Hammer was in the Navy!

Hammer says the time he spent in the Navy was a time he'll never forget — or regret. "In the Navy I learned to be disciplined and detail-oriented. Those are the traits I have used in my business," Hammer explains.

After a three-year tour of duty, Hammer left the Navy at the rank of Petty Officer E-4. Once again, it was time for Hammer to decide what to do with the rest of his life. And once again, the Oakland A's came to his rescue.

3.
Hammerin' Out the Hits!

The first thing M.C. Hammer did when he got out of the Navy was concentrate heavily on Bible studies. He studied six days a week. And for Hammer, it was a natural thing to combine his newfound love for religion with his old-time love of music. So Hammer started writing religious raps. He called himself the Holy Ghost Boy. As the Holy Ghost Boy, Hammer even recorded one gospel rap called "Word." But the tune never made it out of the studio. While that early gospel rap may have never been released, Hammer's kept the feeling alive on his two albums. "Son of the King" is the gospel rap tune on his debut album *Let's Get It Started*. "Pray" is the gospel rap tune on his second super smash album, *Please Hammer Don't Hurt 'Em*.

"I made a commitment a long time ago that I would dedicate one tune on each album to God," Hammer says sincerely. "It's a small way of showing my appreciation. My next album may even have two."

But success wasn't in the cards for the Holy Ghost Boy. Hammer was going to have to make it as M.C. Hammer. So Hammer put together a small posse and started doing less religious raps in the clubs around the Oakland dance club circuit. Hammer was different from the other rappers. Even back in the beginning, Hammer believed that rap could be a lot more than someone standing onstage and bustin' a few rhymes. So he added some slammin' dance moves to his act. The crowds loved him. And Hammer loved the crowds.

"The crowds would go nuts," Hammer says. "I had my whole act choreographed — three young ladies, one guy, myself, and two DJ's. We put on one heck of a show."

Soon it was time for Hammer to put out an album. But Hammer wanted to record his own brand of rap, in his own way. He didn't want to be at the mercy of an established record company, where the producers would try to tell him what to record.

There was only one thing to do. Hammer would have to start his own record label.

But starting your own record label is a lot easier said than done. For one thing, it costs a whole lot of money to rent a recording studio, pay musicians, press your own albums, and make sure those albums get into the record stores. Not many people in East Oakland have that kind of money.

But baseball players do! And two of Hammer's old baseball buddies, Oakland A's Mike Davis and Dwayne Murphy, decided to help the Hammer out. It cost them $20,000 each, but the guys didn't mind. They knew when it came to music, no one could touch the Hammer. Giving Hammer the cash was a safe bet.

Hammer used the money to start Bust It Management/Production. And with the help of producer-musician Felton Pilate, a former member of the rhythm-and-blues group Con Funk Shun, he recorded his first album. The guys recorded the whole album at Fenton's home 16-track recording studio.

"All the vocals were done in a clothes closet," Felton remembers, laughing. "We called it the Incentive Room — the incentive was to hurry up and get the recording done before you burned up in there. But the worst part [about recording in his apartment] was that after ten P.M., the old woman upstairs would pound on my ceiling with a broom any time she heard anything."

All the tough times really paid off. Hammer called his first album *Feel My Power*. And it was a good album, with singles like "Ring 'Em" and "Let's Get It Started." But Hammer soon found out that the difficulties in getting the album recorded were nothing in comparison to getting the album out to the record stores.

This time it was Hammer's new wife, Stephanie, who came to the rescue. She worked day and night, sending promotional tapes of *Feel My Power* to DJ's and radio stations — and calling them to make sure the music got airplay.

At the same time, Hammer was driving all around Oakland, selling *Feel My Power* to small record stores. Violet Brown, an old pal of Hammer's and now a rap music buyer for a chain of record stores on the West Coast, remembers how hard Hammer worked in those early days.

"He's always been quite a businessman," Violet says. "Back then he would sell the albums to all the little mom-and-pop record stores he could. He sold the albums right out of his car trunk."

Hammer's selling strategy worked! *Feel My Power* sold 60,000 copies — and brought him to the attention of Capitol Records. Joy Bailey, an executive at Capitol, heard Hammer at Oakland's Oak Tree Cabaret in May 1988.

"I didn't know who he was at the time," Joy says now. "But watching him, you knew he was going to be somebody!"

With support from Joy, Hammer worked out a $750,000 multi-album deal with Capitol. His next few albums would be joint productions between Bust It and Capitol Records.

Hammer would still be in control, but with Capitol's backing, Hammer could get his music heard all over the world. It was a perfect match.

The first thing Capitol did was rename *Feel My Power*. They called the album *Let's Get It Started*. With the help of tunes like the title track, "Let's Get It Started," and "Pump It Up (Here's the News)," Hammer's debut sold more than a million and a half copies! And the next thing he knew, Hammer was touring the country with a hit album behind him. Hammer and his posse were sharing the stage with rappers like Tone-Lōc, Kool Moe Dee, N.W.A, and Heavy D.

Even though the other acts were more established, it was Hammer who housed them in every stadium! His amazing energy and fancy footwork blew the crowds away. They had never seen steps like Hammer's Chinese Typewriter step (the smooth glide he shows off on the *U Can't Touch This* video) before. And no one could figure out where the Hammer got all that energy. For Hammer, though, getting up the energy was easy. Before each show, Hammer and his posse psyched themselves up the same way.

"All it takes is group prayer, orange juice, and the roar of the crowd," Hammer says. And that's the same method he uses today before each and every show.

Hammer also looked a lot different than the other rappers on the bill. He became famous for wearing loose silk pants and shirts. "At the beginning I had a sense of trying to fit in with the rest of the rap world," Hammer says today. "I dressed like them, but I never started to talk the way rappers tend to talk. There eventually came a time when I said, 'This is not me.' I started upgrading my clothes. When the money came in, the new M.C. Hammer started to unfold."

While he was touring to promote *Let's Get It Started*, Hammer began work on his second album, *Please Hammer Don't Hurt 'Em*. To save time, the hard-working Hammer had his tour bus equipped with $50,000 of recording equipment. He recorded a few of the tunes as his bus rolled from town to town! The album cost Hammer less than $10,000 to record. He's hoping it will sell more than 10 million copies someday!

The rap tunes on *Please Hammer Don't Hurt 'Em* really show Hammer's love of 1970s rhythm and blues. He sampled Rick James's "Super Freak" to give "U Can't Touch This" its pounding hook. He sampled other '70s hits that he remembered loving in his childhood, too.

"I'm twenty-seven years old, and I have a good memory," Hammer says. "When I started recording music, I said, 'I want to do songs like that great music of the seventies. Take, 'Help the Children.' The melody is from Marvin Gaye's 'Mercy Mercy Me.' If you play the two songs side by side, they're similar. But they are also different. Marvin's song *inspired* me."

Hammer's ear for "great music" really paid off. *Please Hammer Don't Hurt 'Em* sold five million copies in less than five months! There was no doubt, Hammer had hit the top.

Still, Hammer wasn't satisfied. He wanted to try something new — making a home video. But Hammer's video wasn't going to be just another collection of his MTV single videos with a few concert shots and interviews stuck in for good measure. Instead, *Please Hammer Don't Hurt 'Em: The Movie* became a full-fledged mini-movie! It tells the story of M.C. Hammer as he returns home to Oakland to go up against a sleazy drug dealer who's dealing to kids. Hammer plays two roles in the video — himself and a rowdy preacher named Reverend Pressure.

Hammer did such a great job playing Reverend Pressure that some people in the movie business are saying that one of these days there just might be a big-screen movie starring M.C. Hammer. And Hammer isn't denying that he'd love that.

"I'm not a singer-turned-want-to-be-movie-star," Hammer insists. "I've always been an actor. The Reverend Pressure parts were all impromptu — there was no script."

But for now, Hammer is concentrating on his European tour. The tour will be similar to his incredible U.S. stage show. Hammer's bringing his 32 dancers and singers with him. And he's sure to use his flashing laser lights and colored smoke screens to show off his feet as he busts those famous Hammer moves! With a wild stage show like M.C. Hammer's, someone better warn Europe — get ready, because now is HAMMER TIME!

4.
Join the Hammer Posse

Imagine you're onstage with M.C. Hammer. It's just you, 32 other dancers and backup singers, and the Hammer himself! Not bad, huh? You'd get to wear those funky, sequined costumes, dance those chill Hammer moves, jam on Hammer's raps, and go around the country housin' every crowd!

Sounds like the perfect life, doesn't it? Well, being part of the Hammer posse isn't as much fun or as easy as it seems. Being part of the Hammer posse is hard work.

First of all, not just anyone can be part of the Hammer posse. "The singers must be talented, and the dancers are required to have the ability to execute intricate dance steps. I also look for team spirit," Hammer explains.

The dancers also have to be creative, since they must come up with a lot of their own fresh dance moves. Hammer does a lot of the choreography for his shows, but everyone gets involved.

"I get a lot of assistance on choreography from one of my groups, Ho Frat Hoo!" Hammer admits. "But everyone onstage pitched in on the development of our current show."

Every single move in the show is calculated down to the smallest kick. And that means a lot of hard work — and a lot of taking orders from M.C. Hammer, without dissin' him!

"Hammer is a former military man, from the Navy," Hammer's brother and manager Louis Burrell says. "He runs a tight ship!"

Tight isn't the word for it. A typical day for the posse starts out early. Even before breakfast, the dancers head out on a four-mile run. Four miles! First thing in the morning!

"Initially, it was tougher on the girls than the guys," Hammer laughs. "That's because the guys had a lot of pride. You know, no matter what, they'd say 'I can do it.' A lot of the girls were ready to just quit. But after a while, they all made it!"

After the run, everyone gets a hearty breakfast — they need it to fuel up for the rest of the day. After breakfast, everyone in the dancing posse goes through a tough weight-lifting routine. After pumping iron, the dancers get down on the ground for a minimum of 300 sit-ups!

Once those tummies have been tightened, the dancers gear up for the real work. The posse is split up into smaller sections. Each section practices its dance routines for a minimum of six hours a day! And there's no slacking off at those rehearsals. Hammer expects everyone to give their all — all the time.

"My rehearsals do leave you slightly tired at the end of the day," Hammer laughs.

But for the most part, the posse members don't mind the workout. "Hammer's strict, but he does it for our own good," Shiralessia Worthen, a dancer in Hammer's show, explains. She says she even looks at Hammer as a substitute "father or big brother. But when he has to, Hammer can get businesslike."

Hammer doesn't ask his posse to do anything he wouldn't do. In fact, believe it or not, Hammer's daily schedule is even busier than that of the dancers. When his posse is on a break, Hammer usually can be found doing interviews with magazines and newspapers, reading through pages and pages of contracts, or planning new jams for that night's show. Since stadiums are different sizes, each new stage means Hammer has to make changes in his show.

"There is no 'typical' day on tour for me," Hammer says. "Each day and each city presents a different challenge and perspective."

But Hammer doesn't mind the work at all. "The best thing about touring is being able to personally deliver my music and my message to my fans," Hammer smiles. "There is nothing bad about touring. I love it!"

And Hammer's fans love him! All that work really pays off. M.C. Hammer shows always give his sold-out audiences more than they could ever ask for. No one in the audience leaves a Hammer show disappointed. Neither do the critics. Hammer gets nothing but rave reviews, no matter where he plays.

"Hammer's dancing acrobatics were astounding as he slid, leaped, crawled, twisted, and shook through roof-raising numbers like 'Turn This Mutha Out,' and 'They Put Me in the Mix,' " *Billboard* magazine wrote of Hammer's 1990 Baltimore jam. And the *Los Angeles Times* called Hammer's August 1990 show at the San Diego Sports Arena "the most furiously entertaining event as might be seen on any California stage this year."

But you can't keep getting reviews like that if you're totally exhausted all the time. That's why Hammer has given everyone in his posse a curfew. After a show, everyone is taken straight back to the hotel. Then, after fifteen minutes in their rooms, it's lights out for everyone.

"We keep a very clean, disciplined organization," Hammer explains. "We have goals, and in order to achieve those goals, we must be disciplined. We don't put curfews on to control everyone's lives. They're the kind of curfews that can save lives. Everybody on the tour is not twenty-five or thirty years old. We've got eighteen- and nineteen-year-olds who we feel responsible for. We allow them to grow up, but we keep everyone out of trouble."

The trouble Hammer is talking about includes messin' with drugs. Anyone caught with drugs on the Hammer tour can forget about being part of the Hammer tour anymore!

Usually, the posse travels from show to show on tour buses. The buses are filled with all sorts of recording equipment, like the equipment Hammer used to record part of *Please Hammer Don't Hurt 'Em* right on his tour bus.

On those nights when the posse has to travel by plane to the next city, Hammer still makes sure everyone gets at least seven hours of sleep. The posse travels by private plane so that Hammer is sure everyone can catch enough z's to make it through the next day.

But not every second on the Hammer tour is filled with sleep and work. There's a lot of laughter, too. And lots of talk about sports — especially about the Oakland A's!

And when Hammer's not leading a rap about his favorite baseball team, he and his posse are looking in the papers for the latest boxing results. Hammer is a *big* boxing fan!

Hammer's other favorite backstage topic is cars. Once Hammer gets talking about wheels, there's no stopping him! The most passed around magazine on the whole tour is the *Du Point Registry* — which is filled with photos and price tags of some of the most expensive cars around!

One of these days Hammer may be driving from gig to gig in his favorite car — a classic Ferrari Testerossa.

"In the beginning I told Capitol that my second album would break all the records for rap records. They said if it did they'd buy me a Ferrari Testerossa. They better be looking for my Testerossa!" Hammer laughs.

But until Capitol picks up the tab for Hammer's $300,000 Ferrari, Hammer will have to be happy traveling from town to town in private planes and tour buses with his hard-working posse.

5.
The Rappers Are All Rappin' About Hammer!

You don't get to be as big as M.C. Hammer without somebody dissin' you about something. In Hammer's case, it's not the record companies, the audiences, the critics, or even the censorship groups that are doing the dissin'. Hammer's only critics are his fellow rappers.

As soon as *Please Hammer Don't Hurt 'Em* started racing up the charts, the other rappers started hurting the Hammer. They started calling him things like "M.C. Sellout" because his music crossed the line between black rap and white pop. Some hardcore rap magazines aren't in Hammer's corner, either. *The Source*, rap's leading magazine, won't even list *Please Hammer Don't Hurt 'Em* on its album chart. An article in the magazine even went so far as to call Hammer's rappin': "a cheesy, pop-oriented production. His rhymes are as creative as a glass of warm milk!"

And West Coast rapper Ice-T dissed Hammer even harder than that! At the New Music Seminar's 1990 Rap Music Summit, Ice-T announced, "Hammer's cool, but he's not hip-hop!"

But Hammer doesn't think of himself as a crossover artist. He doesn't think of himself as a musician in any category. He's just playing his own music for whoever wants to listen. And if that includes both black and white b-boys and b-girls, that's even better.

"Other rappers think any time the public at large embraces rap, then the rap is no good. But I have never succumbed to peer pressure and that's why I am M.C. Hammer," Hammer defends himself. "I never strayed [from rap]. I merely expanded and innovated the rap market. I brought entertainment back to the stage."

But there are a lot of rappers out there who don't think rap should be pure entertainment. They see rap as more of a political message about black power.

"People say Hammer lacks consciousness, street depth, and basically any contact with the black public," Mike Mosbe, the host of the syndicated rap program *Hip-Hop Countdown and Report* says.

But Hammer hasn't lost touch with the black public at all. And his actions speak a lot louder than most rappers' words. Hammer doesn't have much free time to spend at home in Oakland. When he's there he'd like to spend the time with his two-year-old daughter, Akeiba Monique. But when he's home, you're more than likely to find the city's hottest homie roamin' the halls of the city's schools talking to underprivileged kids. "I make an active effort to remain a positive role model to kids," Hammer says sincerely. "They need people to show them there's another way."

Whenever Hammer visits the schools, he always gives the kids the same message. "I tell them to stay in school, stay away from drugs, obey your parents, and trust in God."

And when it comes to helping kids, Hammer puts his money where his mouth is. A big part of the money from his *Help the Children* video went straight into Hammer's newly founded Help the Children Foundation. The foundation is dedicated to making sure the kids follow Hammer's advice and stay straight and in school.

While not even the nastiest rapper could argue with Hammer's charity work, lots of them find fault with the rhymes he's been bustin'. Hammer's words are the cleanest in rap. And no matter what the other rappers say, Hammer intends to keep them that way.

"There definitely is a need for more positive role models [in rap]," Hammer says. "I believe that there are more positive ways to convey a message without the use of excessive profanity and/or suggestiveness."

Hammer's clean-cut rhymes and shows aren't just some act to make him appeal to grown-up audiences. It's just the way Hammer is. Hammer's longtime pal, record store rap music buyer Violet Brown, remembers one time she invited Hammer to one of her record stores to sign records, CD's, and cassettes.

"One time I asked him to do an in-store visit," Violet recalls. "While he was there, someone put on a song with cursing on it. Hammer stopped everything and screamed from the back of the store, 'I won't have that kind of language while I'm here and all these kids are here! Turn that record off!' He really is as clean as he seems. In all the time I've known Hammer I've never heard him curse. He doesn't smoke and he drinks nothing but orange juice, no alcohol." Violet is also quick to jump to her pal's defense. "The rappers that say things about Hammer are just jealous. They should be grateful to Hammer. He's opening up the market for rap music. He's getting rap a place on white radio stations!"

Even though M.C. Hammer's lyrics are clean, he defends other rappers who have gotten into trouble for their rough lyrics.

"I'm against censorship," Hammer says defiantly. "But I do feel that warning labels would give parents the option of regulating what their children are exposed to."

Hammer admits his top priority is today's kids. But he does a lot of great things for adults who are in trouble, too. A lot of the workers at his management company, Bust It Management/Production are people who are just out of prison. "[Hiring people who have been in prison] is just my own small way of trying to correct society's reluctance to give a person a second chance," he says simply.

Whether or not other rappers agree with Hammer's music, they did get together with him in a special effort to stop gang wars in Los Angeles. Last summer, 14 West Coast rappers, including Hammer, Tone-Lōc, Young MC, and Def Jeff, got together to record a single called "We're All in the Same Gang." The song rapped about staying out of gangs. Part of the money from the single went to Project Build, a Los Angeles group that is dedicated to keeping Los Angeles teens in school.

Hammer was glad he could get together with other rappers to help California kids. The project was right up his alley. After all, one of Hammer's main goals in life is to give back some of the wonderful things that have been given to him.

As he says: "I want to be remembered as a positive role model who tried to give back to the community love and respect."

6.
It's an M.C. Hammer
Quickie Quiz!

How big a Hammer fan are you? Only M.C. Hammer's deffest fans can nail these Hammer trivia questions. (Answers on page 40.)

1. What baseball player gave M.C. Hammer the nickname "Little Hammer"?
   A. Vida Blue
   B. Henry Aaron
   C. Pedro Garcia

2. True or false: M.C. Hammer was once in the Marines.

3. "U Can't Touch This" samples its strong riff from "Super Freak." Who wrote "Super Freak"?
   A. Rick James
   B. M.C. Hammer
   C. Chuck D.

4. What is the name of the music company M.C. Hammer started?
   A. Hip-Hop Records
   B. Bust It Management/Production
   C. Hammer Productions

5. True or false: The name of Hammer's first album was *It's Hammer Time!*

6. Part of the money earned from M.C. Hammer's *Help the Children* video will go to what charity?
   A. The Help the Children Foundation
   B. UNICEF
   C. Greenpeace

7. True or false: The Hammer posse practices dancing for 10 hours a day.

8. What is the name of the gospel rap on *Please Hammer Don't Hurt 'Em*?
   A. "Pray"
   B. "Thank You"
   C. "Grace"

9. True or false: Because of his dancing, M.C. Hammer is often called "the Paula Abdul of rap."

10. The melody of "Help the Children" is taken from what 1970s song?
    A. "Mercy Mercy Me"
    B. "Hotel California"
    C. "The Pretender"

11. What was the name of the Baptist minister Hammer played in his *Please Hammer Don't Hurt 'Em* video?
    A. Reverend Hammer
    B. Reverend Treasure
    C. Reverend Pressure

12. What is the name of Hammer's daughter?
    A. Keisha
    B. Mary
    C. Akeiba

13. When Oakland A's owner Charlie O. Finley discovered Hammer in the A's parking lot, Hammer was doing routines based on which musician's songs?
    A. Marvin Gaye
    B. James Brown
    C. Little Richard

14. True or false: *Please Hammer Don't Hurt 'Em* cost less than $10,000 to record.

15. When Hammer went to college, what did he major in?
    A. Music
    B. Math
    C. Communications

16. What was the original title of *Let's Get It Started*?
    A. *Feel My Power*
    B. *Let's Get It Started*
    C. *The Fresh Album*

17. True or false: Hammer doesn't need glasses to see; he just wears them to look cool.

18. What was the name of the collection of rappers that recorded "We're All in the Same Gang"?
    A. Rapper Posse
    B. Rapper Gang
    C. West Coast Rap All-Stars

19. What soda did M.C. Hammer promote?
    A. Coke
    B. Pepsi
    C. RC Cola

20. What position did Hammer hold with the Oakland A's?
    A. Right field
    B. Catcher
    C. Batboy

ANSWERS

1. C
2. False, he was in the Navy.
3. A
4. B
5. False, it was *Let's Get It Started*.
6. A
7. False, only six hours.
8. A
9. True
10. A (by Marvin Gaye)
11. C
12. C
13. B
14. True
15. C
16. A
17. False
18. C
19. B
20. C

VANILLA ICE

THE MAKING OF A RAP STAR!

1.
The Iceman Burns Up the Charts!

"By the end of this last tour I wasn't really opening for Hammer anymore, he was kind of closing for me. No, I mean it! There were people in the audiences who had driven three hundred miles just to see me. It kind of blew me away!"

When Vanilla Ice says things like that, he's not dissin' the Hammer. He's just telling the truth as he sees it. The fact is, no one in rap history has ever had the rapid surefire success of this rapper from Florida! And by the end of last year's M.C. Hammer tour, in which Vanilla Ice was signed on as an opening act, there were just as many Vanilla Ice fans in the audience as there were Hammer fans!

Vanilla Ice has been causing chart meltdown with his first album, *To the Extreme*, ever since it was released September 18, 1990. In less than two months, the album sold two million copies! According to officials at SBK Records, Vanilla Ice's label, the record company worked day and night and still couldn't press enough albums, CD's, and cassettes to keep record stores around the country stocked. At its peak, *To the Extreme* was selling 250,000 copies a day! That was enough to melt away all of Vanilla Ice's competition — including M.C. Hammer. By Halloween night, Vanilla Ice nailed the Hammer on the head and knocked *Please Hammer Don't Hurt 'Em* out of the *Billboard* number one album spot — a place the M.C. Hammer album had held for more than three months! Not a bad 22nd birthday present. Ice's birthday is October 31.

The first single from the album, "Ice Ice Baby," shot like a rocket to the number one position on the *Billboard* rap chart — blowing veteran rapper L.L. Cool J out of the top spot. The single also made it all the way to the number eight spot on *Billboard*'s R&B charts. But the biggest break came in October 1990, when "Ice Ice Baby" became the first rap single ever to crash into the number one position on the *Billboard* Hot 100!

But the success hasn't changed Vanilla Ice at all. According to a representative of Shock Ink, his management company, Ice is still the laid-back homie he always was.

"On his birthday, SBK threw him a huge party," the representative says. "Vanilla Ice couldn't believe it was all for him! And when he was presented with a double platinum album, well, I think he was in shock!"

Vanilla Ice isn't the only one in shock these days. The folks at SBK Records are pretty amazed themselves. "We never could have predicted this," Daniel Glass, senior vice-president in charge of promotion for SBK says. "You can never predict a phenomenon. We knew we had a catchy record in 'Ice Ice Baby.' But who would have expected this kind of success!"

There's more to Vanilla Ice's popularity than just his music. There's his dancing, too. Ice makes up all of his own dances, and personally teaches all the steps to the dancing members of the VIP's (Vanilla Ice Posse). His funky footwork helped make sure the video for "Ice Ice Baby" entered the MTV Video countdown at number 13 and kept on climbing! The video was also the most requested video on *Video Jukebox* for nine consecutive weeks!

But the place Vanilla Ice really shines is onstage. When he and his posse break into raps like "Stop That Train" and "Play That Funky Music," no one in the house can stay seated. Ice's hard-hitting rap style and icy smooth dance moves drag everyone into the groove! Before you know it, the crowd is dancing in the aisles and bustin' rhymes along with Vanilla Ice. By the end of the set, the crowd is screaming for more. And that's okay by Vanilla Ice; he'd be glad to "Play That Funky Music" all night long! There's no place Vanilla Ice would rather be than on the stage!

"The best part about being on tour is getting on that stage," he says. "That's what we all came here for. And when I heard the crowd screaming for more, it just feels amazing!"

Now, with a top-selling home video, a lead role in *Teenage Mutant Ninja Turtles Part II*, and a single from the movie, Vanilla Ice has been frozen into instant stardom! Nothing can stop him now. All this success has left Vanilla Ice a little blown away.

"I was struggling along for about three years, and now, suddenly, everything has just EXPLODED! My career went from one place to outer space! I am shocked! It's taken me totally by surprise. It's taken everyone by surprise. Even Hammer. Backstage one night Hammer just turned to me and said 'Man, I can't touch you! I can't touch you!' "

These days, it seems like nobody can touch Vanilla Ice!

2.
A Rap Star Grows Up

The Vanilla Ice story starts in an area of Florida called Miami Lakes, on Halloween night in 1968. That's the night the little baby who would grow up to be rap sensation Vanilla Ice was born. Like any baby, Ice came out screaming. But nobody in that hospital room could have predicted how important that set of lungs was going to wind up being to rap history!

As a kid, Ice grew up in a small house with his mother, his older brother, and his baby sister. Ice's father left home while he was really young, so the rapper doesn't talk about him much.

Oh, and just in case you hadn't already guessed, Vanilla Ice isn't the cool rap star's real name. He was born Robert Van Winkle. He didn't get his nickname until much later. Vanilla Ice says that he got his stage handle from some of the black kids who lived in the projects near his house.

"The projects were near my house," he explains, "and that's where my friends were from. By seventh grade I was already a rapper, and the kids on the street would look at my complexion and say, 'Yo! You're vanilla!' I would tell the kids rhymes and stuff off the top of my head and someone said, 'Aw man, that's ice! That's smooth! A cold rap!' After that, I was always Vanilla Ice."

Considering Ice was born in Florida, that was some compliment! After all, Florida has launched some of rap's hottest groups, including the controversial 2 Live Crew. 2 Live Crew has had its share of problems. Their tough lyrics have led them to trouble in the courts, because some people think 2 Live Crew's music is obscene. But unlike 2 Live Crew, Vanilla Ice has always made sure his lyrics are free of curse words. To this day, you won't hear any cursing on a Vanilla Ice album.

"There are a lot of kids out there who look up to me, follow me," Ice says. "I want to be a positive model for them!"

Still, Ice doesn't think 2 Live Crew is getting a fair deal. Vanilla Ice is completely against censoring rap groups (or anyone for that matter) — but that doesn't mean he doesn't think there should be warning labels on all kinds of record albums. He does. The labels would tell parents that some of the language on the record might be considered offensive. "I think parents should have some control over their kids," he says.

As a kid, Vanilla Ice's house was always filled with music. His older brother spent a lot of time trying to turn Ice on to rock and roll, but Ice wouldn't even listen to it.

"I don't listen to that stuff at all!" Vanilla Ice says defiantly. "When my brother was listening to rock and roll, I was listening to funk! Now I mostly listen to rap and reggae. The only reason I would ever listen to rock and roll now is to get ideas for raps."

While Ice's brother was trying to get Ice to appreciate rock and roll, Ice's mother was trying to get him to spend some of his time practicing classical music on the piano. Ice's mother is a classical musician who teaches flute, piano, and voice. Unfortunately, her youngest son had no interest in sitting down at the piano and practicing his scales.

"I just couldn't take the time out to sit and do it. But my mom sure did try to teach me!" Ice laughs.

Actually, as a kid Ice wasn't really interested in becoming a musician at all. When he rapped, he just rapped for fun. What Ice really wanted to do was to race motorcycles professionally in the Moto-cross!

"I was racing in the Moto-cross when I was four years old," Ice says proudly. "It was my whole life. I really thought that was what I wanted to be!"

And Ice was good at racing. He was a regular on the amateur circuit by the time he was 15. "I'd get to the racetrack and know I was going to win!" Ice says confidently.

Vanilla Ice did drop out of high school at age 15 to go out on the Moto-cross circuit. But he got his diploma anyway, through a correspondence course with the American School. Ice thinks all rappers should finish high school. "You can't speak knowledge if you don't have knowledge," he says. By finishing school through the mail, Ice got his knowledge, and had the freedom to ride his bike.

Vanilla Ice is quick to tell you that racing gave him more than just thrills. It kept him away from drugs. And in Ice's neighborhood, drugs were always around.

"Moto-cross is a great sport because it keeps kids off of drugs," he says seriously. "It keeps kids off the streets. If a kid is into motorcycle racing, his parents should support him all the way. It will keep him off of drugs."

Still, the Moto-cross couldn't keep Ice completely out of trouble. He spent a lot of his teenage years fighting in a gang.

"I got stabbed five times," he says, slowly. "The last time was when I was eighteen. I lost half the blood out of my body. When I woke up I felt as if God had given me a second chance. That was four years ago. Since then I've prayed every single day at least twice."

After the stabbing, Ice quit the gang and spent all of his time racing. Actually, it was because of the Moto-cross that Ice started taking rapping seriously. In 1987, Ice was in a serious motorcycle accident. He broke both of his ankles. He had to have two painful operations and still his doctors told him there was an 80 percent chance he would never walk again!

But Ice wasn't going to spend the rest of his life in a wheelchair. He fought like mad to prove those doctors wrong.

"It was tough!" Ice says. "I spent six weeks in a hospital. Then I had to go through really painful physical therapy. But it was worth it. Now my ankles work perfectly and I can dance better than ever!"

Even though his ankles turned out good as new, the accident did change Ice's life forever. He began to devote more of his time to rap. He practiced his dance moves for hours on end, and spent night after night busting new rhymes at house parties. He started entering rap talent contests all over the Miami area. Then one night, while he was on vacation in Dallas, Texas, a buddy dared him to enter a contest in a local club. And the rest, as they say, is history!

3.
A Little Texas Luck

While Ice's ankles were on the mend, he
and a few of his biking buddies decided to
take off for Dallas, Texas. There Ice could
get a much needed vacation. For the most
part, this was an ordinary vacation, a
bunch of guys spending most of their nights
hanging out at the local rap clubs in the
Dallas/Fort Worth area. Then one night,
something special happened. Something so
special that it would make Cinderella's
night with the prince seem like no big deal.
In that one magical night, a motorcycle
racer from Florida became a professional
rapper!

The way Ice tells it, he and a pal wan-
dered into a Dallas club called City Lights.
Just for fun, Ice's buddy entered him into
a rap showdown contest.

"I was competing against bands that took hours just to set up their equipment," Ice says. "The organizers asked me what I needed. I said, 'Just a microphone, that's all!' Then I grabbed ahold of the mike and busted a rhyme right there, right off the top of my head. The crowd started clapping with the rhyme, and everyone was going kind of crazy."

When Ice was through rapping, the crowd wouldn't let him off the stage. So just for laughs he started busting a beat box (making drum sounds with his mouth).

"That's when everyone started rushing the stage and yelling and stuff," Ice recalls. That was Ice's big chance to show off his other talent — dancing!

"I just told the crowd, 'First you heard me bust a rhyme, then you heard me bust a beat. Now check it out, I'm gonna move my feet.' " Then, with only that warning, Ice broke into one of his jammin' dance routines! That was all it took. After that performance, Ice not only won the contest, he gained an agent and the respect of several talent scouts.

"I guess I really lucked out," Ice says now, looking back on that night. "I mean, here I was in Dallas, in this club I had never been in before, won a local talent contest, and I didn't find out until after it was all over that there were people from Warner Brothers, Motown, and MCA in the audience. They were all out there in the crowd. I signed with my agent the very next day."

Ice's new agent, Tommy Quon, got busy getting his client paying gigs. In the next two and a half years, Ice shared the stage with almost every rap act around — including N.W.A, Eazy-E, the D.O.C., Sir Mix-A-Lot, and Cash Money.

Being an opening act for a big star is no easy task. The audience isn't there to see some new kid, they're there to see the headliner. Sometimes the audience can get pretty rough — booing and throwing things at the opening acts. If that weren't tough enough, some people thought that the audience would have trouble with the fact that Ice was a white rapper. But Ice wasn't concerned. He knew once the audience heard him bust a few rhymes and watched him do some slammin' dance moves, he'd win them over. So every night, Ice just went out there on the stage and did what he does best — rap!

"I wasn't worried," Ice says. "The way rap audiences operate, you just have to prove yourself. You have to be sincere and earn respect. If I had come on real weak or something — like New Kids on the Block trying to do rap — the audience would know that was commercial, not straight from the heart. The audiences liked the jam. They didn't care if I was black or white!"

Black or white, very few people have the star quality Vanilla Ice has. "You can just feel it when he walks in a room," SBK's Daniel Glass explains. "You walk in a restaurant with him and people want his autograph. They don't even have to know who he is." It is that star quality that carried Vanilla Ice through those early days when no one in the audience knew anything about him or his music.

Besides the touring, Ice flew off to Atlanta and entered a small recording studio. It was time to cut his first album. In the recording studio, Ice pushed aside some veteran rap producers and really took over. Ice didn't just do the rhyming. He was involved in every aspect of the album's production. He wrote all of the lyrics (although he admits to busting a few of the rhymes right off the top of his head while the tape was rolling), and produced or co-produced all of the songs on the album.

"When you hear Vanilla Ice, you hear Vanilla Ice," Ice explains. "That's who I am, no phoniness. My music is the straight-up truth! I write my own lyrics and produce my own songs."

Ice did have some help in the studio, though. When you play the album, you can hear the masterful mixing of sounds by Ice's DJ and soundman, Earthquake.

Ice and Earthquake put nine tunes together and called the album *Hooked*. *Hooked* was distributed by a small label, Ultrax Records. The first single from *Hooked* was "Play That Funky Music." On the flip side was a little rap called "Ice Ice Baby." It was a DJ in Chattanooga, Tennessee, who decided to flip the record over and play "Ice Ice Baby" on the radio. Almost immediately, "Ice Ice Baby" jumped to number one in Chattanooga, and then to number one in Dallas.

"We sold forty thousand copies of *Hooked* in three months," Ice says, "and major record companies started calling."

That's when SBK Records entered the picture. They bought the rights to *Hooked*. Ice added a few new raps and renamed the album *To the Extreme*. SBK rereleased

"Ice Ice Baby" with a radio mix, and a special extra-danceable club mix. That was all the push the single needed to jump it to number one nationwide.

Hooked was one smart buy for SBK! In fact, Vanilla Ice's red-hot success was one of the main reasons SBK's Chief Executive Officer, Charles Koppelman, was named to *Entertainment* Magazine's list of the top 101 people in the entertainment business. "His ear for talent has made [SBK] respected," the magazine said about Charles Koppelman. "In 1990, SBK has been on a winning streak, including the Wilson Phillips debut and the stunning successes of Technotronic and Vanilla Ice."

To many people in the rap world it seemed as though Ice was an overnight success. But the DJ's in the rap clubs around the country knew better.

"Vanilla Ice may have surprised some people, but not me," Violet Brown, a rap record buyer for a chain of record stores in California, and a DJ in the Los Angeles area, says. "I've been a DJ for a lot of clubs and parties here. That record ["Ice Ice Baby"] had been around for a while before it became number one. Everytime I would put it on, people loved it."

Ice himself thinks that it's the press that has turned him into some sort of "overnight" sensation. "It sure wasn't overnight," he says. "I've been rapping since the seventh grade. And I struggled for almost three years as a professional. That's a long time to struggle."

By the end of the summer of 1990, Ice's struggle was just about over — thanks to a tour with veteran rapper M.C. Hammer!

4.
Hitting the Road with Hammer!

In the summer of 1990, nobody in the music business was bigger than M.C. Hammer. His second album, *Please Hammer Don't Hurt 'Em* had been number one on the charts for months. Nobody could touch the Hammer!

When Vanilla Ice signed on to tour with Hammer, he was thrilled. M.C. Hammer had a crossover audience. The people who went to Hammer shows weren't only rap fans, they were pop fans, too. Now Vanilla Ice could show off his stuff to a whole new audience!

Although Ice had toured before, nothing could prepare him for the stress and strain of the Hammer tour. The tour started up on September 19 in Cedar Rapids, Iowa, and before he knew it, Ice was zigzagging around the country in his private plane for almost three full months!

Ice certainly wasn't lonely while he was on tour. He flew from city to city in his plane with eight members of the Vanilla Ice Posse (VIP's) — his road manager, his dancers, his DJ, and others who helped the tour run smoothly. He took a private plane mostly because it was more convenient than taking regular commercial flights. In order to make it to a lot of his dates, Ice has to be able to fly off at a moment's notice. It's impossible to do that on a regular airline. Also, private planes are much more comfortable to travel in than regular passenger planes. Ice's plane has stereo systems, a full kitchen, and places for Ice and the VIP members to catch up on some much needed sleep. Ice's plane is sort of like a flying hotel room!

It's a good thing the plane is so comfortable, because the only time Ice ever has a chance to get any sleep while on tour is on the plane.

"Being on tour means always being busy," he laughs. "I never get any sleep. I mean NO sleep! And some days, I don't even have time to get my clothes cleaned. Here I am in all these great cities and I never have a chance to shop. I just go from one city to the next."

And sleep isn't the only thing Vanilla Ice misses while he's on tour. He also misses his family. He rarely gets to talk to his mother, and he speaks to his brother and sister even less.

"It's not that we're not close," he says. "I've just been on the road for a long time, and there's no time to just talk."

There's no such thing as a typical tour day for Vanilla Ice. His schedule changes from city to city. But one thing's for sure — he's always kept on the run.

"Now, take today," he says from his hotel room. "We just got off the plane and rushed off to the hotel. I barely had a chance to wash my face. Now I'm talkin' to y'all. But there's two video crews — one from *Smash Hits* and one from MTV waiting downstairs to do interviews. Then I have an interview with someone from *Vanity Fair* magazine. Then I've got to get in the car and get over to the concert hall. Then it's time for the sound check, because I always want everything to sound perfect. Then we've all got to take showers, grab a quick bite to eat, and get on that stage!"

Whew! With days like that, it's a wonder Vanilla Ice has any strength to make those dancing videos like *Ice Ice Baby*! "I made the video before I started the Hammer tour," he laughs.

To the outsider it seems that there's nothing in this world that could make a schedule like Vanilla Ice's worthwhile. Still Ice is out there jammin' every night. And he says he wouldn't trade this life for anything! First of all, there's a lot of money involved. Ice won't talk about how much he makes per show on the Hammer tour, but odds are it's a lot more cash than he could get on a Moto-cross tour. And there's the chance for Ice to learn from rap's number one performer, M.C. Hammer.

"I learn more from Hammer every day," Ice says. "You can learn so much just by watching him onstage." But more than the money or the lessons, Ice stays on the road because he loves rappin'!

"My heart is in rap music," he explains. "And I love being onstage. That's my favorite part. That's what we all came here for."

And the audiences love having Ice onstage. By the middle of the Hammer tour, *To the Extreme* had blasted its way to number one. The audience knew all of his tunes, and they were jammin' along with Vanilla Ice when he rapped.

"Actually, Vanilla Ice is a better rapper than Hammer," record buyer and DJ Violet Brown says. "And he's got some good dance moves. I think he's getting quite popular with the ladies."

But it's not just the fly girls in the audience that watch Vanilla Ice. Both the guys and the girls in Ice's audiences are always waiting to see if this will be the night that Ice will do the one thing he keeps promising to try — riding onstage on his motorcycle and popping a wheelie. So far, he hasn't.

"I'm not sure I'll be able to do it on this tour. But one of these days, I just might pull a bike out there," he says. "You never know."

In the meantime, Vanilla Ice is having a tough enough time just keeping up with his schedule. But being busy doesn't keep Ice from paying back the people for having made him so popular. Last October, he actually took a night off from the Hammer tour. But Ice didn't spend the night chillin' out from the tour. Instead Vanilla Ice flew up to Boston to play at a benefit to help abused children.

"I took a night off from a paying gig and played the rally for free. It felt great to help the kids. A lot of people have helped me along the way. I think it's really important to give something back. I'm just a good guy, I guess!"

Spoken like a true homeboy!

5.
Fresh Stuff
from Vanilla Ice!

How to top 1990? That was the big question on Vanilla Ice's mind by the time late November rolled around. After all, not many rappers get an out-of-the-box year like his. Top album, top video, sold-out shows. What next? Who knows?

The first thing Ice did was make sure sales of *To the Extreme* stayed frozen at the top of the charts. He put together his first home video, *Play That Funky Music*. The video was made up of Ice's already released videos: *Play That Funky Music*, *Stop That Train*, and *Ice Ice Baby*. It also featured an up-close interview of the Iceman himself! The video was released just in time for the Christmas rush. Lots of rappers unwrapped Ice's video at Christmastime. Just like his album, Ice's video was a big seller!

Along with the Christmas release of the video, SBK rereleased "Play That Funky Music" as Ice's new single. The record company is planning to follow up "Play That Funky Music" with the single release of "Stop That Train." That should keep *To the Extreme* at the top for a long time!

In early November 1990, Vanilla Ice took a few weeks off from the Hammer tour to head down to North Carolina and film his part in *Teenage Mutant Ninja Turtles Part II*.

According to SBK's Daniel Glass, Ice was originally only supposed to write one song for the movie. But as the filming date for *Teenage Mutant Ninja Turtles Part II* grew near, Ice started to become hotter and hotter. Suddenly, the movie company decided to give Ice a big acting role in the film. It was the first time Ice had ever acted.

Luckily, the part wasn't much of a stretch for him. He got to play the part of a rapper named Jack, who meets the Turtles while he's bustin' rhymes in a club. At one point in the movie, the Turtles get in trouble and it's Vanilla Ice to the rescue!

"I'd never acted before," Ice says. "But everyone said I was going to be great. All I had to be was myself. That's what I did!"

One thing nobody told Ice was that he would have more free time on the movie set than he'd had all year. That's because movies are filmed very slowly. Sometimes there are hours of time between takes. For someone who's on the go as much as Ice, that time could drive you crazy. But Ice got smart. He used that time to record a rap for the movie. It's called "Ninja Rap."

Ice is hoping that the success of *Teenage Mutant Ninja Turtles Part II* (which is supposed to be in the theaters by late March 1991) will send him off on a chillin' movie career. The first Turtles movie earned 130 million dollars in the theaters. That doesn't even include the more than seven million videocassettes of the movie that were sold!

"Movies are definitely in the future and the Teenage Mutant Ninja Turtles movie is a definite start," he says. "But rap is still number one for me!"

To prove it, Ice has started recording his second album. Some people in the record business say he may have to soften his hard-edged rap to please the younger kids who will discover him in the Turtles movie. But Ice definitely doesn't agree. He's pretty sure kids of all ages will like his own style of rap. Right now, Ice won't say much about the new album except that it is going to have the same hard-hitting, straight from the streets feel *To the Extreme* has.

"Let's be honest," he says. "To really rap, you need to know how to rap, not just bust words that rhyme. I mean using street terminology, stuff people on the street can understand. That's where I'm coming from. That's the rap that's in my heart."

Now that the United States has developed Ice fever, Vanilla Ice has decided to take his beat over to Europe. Just after he finished filming *Teenage Mutant Ninja Turtles Part II*, Vanilla Ice flew over to England to debut "Ice Ice Baby" on *Smash Hits*, the number one music show in England. After that Ice took a quick hop over to Germany, just to bring the Germans some hip-hop!

But Ice didn't forget the U.S. In January, he started rehearsals for his own U.S. tour — and this time Ice was the headliner!

With all that fame and fortune, you'd think that Vanilla Ice wouldn't want to help any new rappers get started on their own def careers. But you'd be wrong. Ice has some real straight advice for young rappers.

"If you're true to yourself, and you have faith you can make it, then stick behind the rap one hundred percent! Enter any contest you can; just make yourself seen! I'm talkin' any talent contest. Even if you have to drive a hundred miles. Just get in a car and do it. Remember how I lucked out in Dallas!"

Sounds like good advice. It sure worked for Vanilla Ice. His music train is definitely rolling, and for now anyway, it looks like nothing can Stop That Train!

6.
It's a Vanilla Ice Quickie Quiz!

How much do you know about Vanilla Ice? Can you melt through these hot questions about one cool rapper? (Answers on page 76.)

1. What is the name of the company that publishes Vanilla Ice's music?
   A. Ice Baby Music
   B. Vanilla Tunes
   C. Cold Rap Music

2. "Vanilla Ice" is only a nickname. What is the Iceman's real name?
   A. Abraham Van Helsing
   B. Robert Van Winkle
   C. Steven Krommenhoek

3. At what Dallas club did Vanilla Ice cause a sensation and gain an agent?
    A. City Lights
    B. Rapper's Domain
    C. The Gold Chain

4. What tune does Vanilla Ice sample on "Ice Ice Baby"?
    A. "Under Pressure"
       by David Bowie and Queen
    B. "Birthday" by the Beatles
    C. "What's Goin' On"
       by Marvin Gaye

5. Name the song Vanilla Ice wrote for *Teenage Mutant Ninja Turtles Part II*.
    A. "Your Shell or Mine"
    B. "Turtle Terror"
    C. "Ninja Rap"

6. Which of the following did Vanilla Ice *not* tour with?
    A. Sir Mix-A-Lot
    B. Whitney Houston
    C. Ice-T

7. Name Vanilla Ice's record company.
   A. Capitol Records
   B. SBK Records
   C. Epic Records

8. What is the name of Vanilla Ice's DJ?
   A. Earthquake
   B. Black Lightening
   C. Cool D.

9. True or false: As part of his stage act, Vanilla Ice jumps up and hangs from specially made rafters above the stage.

10. Name the correspondence school where Vanilla Ice finished high school.
    A. The American School
    B. The Professional Children's School
    C. The Scholastic Aptitude School

11. True or false: "Play That Funky Music" is sampled from a tune by a group called Wild Cherry.

12. True or false: Vanilla Ice has an older sister.

13. True or false: Vanilla Ice was born on Thanksgiving Day.

14. Which of these songs is *not* on *To the Extreme*?
    A. "Life Is a Fantasy"
    B. "Cold Rap"
    C. "Rosta Man"

15. Besides rap, what is Vanilla Ice's favorite type of music?
    A. Reggae
    B. Classical
    C. Heavy metal

ANSWERS

1. A
2. B
3. A
4. A
5. C
6. B
7. B
8. A
9. False
10. A
11. True
12. False. He has a younger sister and an older brother.
13. False. He was born on Halloween.
14. B
15. A